WHOLE LOTTA CREATIVITY

GOING ON:

60

FUN AND UNUSUAL EXERCISES
TO AWAKEN AND STRENGTHEN
YOUR CREATIVITY

By

Regina Pacelli

ISBN-13: 978-1490921785

ISBN-10: 1490921788

WHOLE LOTTA CREATIVITY GOING ON:

60 FUN AND UNUSUAL EXERCISES

TO AWAKEN AND STRENGTHEN

YOUR CREATIVITY

TABLE OF CONTENTS

How to Use this Book

Whole Lotta Creativity Going On: 60 Fun and Unusual Exercises to Awaken and Strengthen Your Creativity is intended to be a fun way to give your creative side a little boost. Some of the exercises are also meant to deepen your awareness of the world around you, enhancing your way of seeing things, which will in turn help to fuel your ability to think creatively.

I believe that everyone is creative. Everyone! It's just that sometimes that side hasn't been given enough of an opportunity to flourish.

This book consists of 60 exercises, some of them on the usual side, which are divided into 10 categories (listed later in this section). Each category focuses on a different aspect of creativity, but be aware that the categories are not all-encompassing since the topic of creativity as a whole is much broader than the slice of exercises contained in the book. Also, you should be aware that this is *NOT* a how-to book, so it does not contain any discussions or tutorials on the topic.

Most of the exercises come with rules to keep things focused, but if a particular rule is not feasible in your situation, then modify it and put "your own creative spin" on it. You can do one activity or exercise a day or one a week, whatever works best for you.

The table of contents is organized in such a way that you get a mixture of categories as you progress in exercise number order. However, all of the exercises are stand-alone and do not need to be done in any particular sequence, so if you prefer instead to do all of a particular category as a set, you can easily pick them out from the table of contents (which lists the category next to each exercise number).

The exercises will take varying amounts of time to plan out or execute. Some are simple in that they require no planning or preparation; others will require a certain amount of forethought. If you prefer, you can keep some in planning mode until you are ready to execute them, while you proceed with the other shorter, easier ones in the meantime.

Some you may find easy, others may be a stretch for you because maybe it's exercising an area that you have not really had the opportunity to develop or had much exposure to. But, no worries! There are no right or wrong answers, no good or bad outcomes or conclusions. As you go through the exercises in the book, you should keep the following thought in your mind: that every step you take and every attempt you make is further honing and strengthening your abilities, and that is the goal – to use them as a springboard for developing your creative muscles and becoming a more creative you (and to have some fun along the way!).

The exercises fall into the following categories:

1. Awareness, Sensory, and Experience
2. Creativity in Action
3. Ideation
4. Imagination
5. Pictures, Patterns, and Abstractions
6. Snap Portraits
7. Snap Solutions
8. Stop and Reflect
9. Thought Expression
10. Word Play.

Enjoy!

THE EXERCISES

Exercise 1: Imagination

Megan, who is deathly afraid of heights, allowed herself to be convinced to go along with some friends on a hot air balloon ride. She got in and shut her eyes tight.

Describe what takes place in the minutes that follow.

Exercise 2: Ideation

A woman in an expensive blue dress ran out of a restaurant and got into a cab which then raced away.

Come up with at least twenty (20) possible "completely different from each other" explanations why she left in such a hurry.

Exercise 3: Awareness, Sensory, and Experience

Spend part of the day (at least a couple of hours) communicating and having conversations with others ONLY through body language and pantomime.

Suggestions: tell them about your day; tell them a story; teach them something; ask them a question or answer one; discuss something with them, or work on a joint task together.

Reflect on how it went. Was it smooth sailing or were there issues, and if so, what were they? Think about how to overcome them and try the exercise again on another day.

Exercise 4: Thought Expression

Come up with four different definitions for what the phrase "early to the vine" could possibly mean.

The first definition should be believable; the second should be witty; the third should evoke thoughts of peacefulness, and the fourth should be utterly outlandish.

Exercise 5: Snap Solutions

You're the owner of a small grocery store. Recently, business has been getting worse. Many of your customers are now going to the much larger grocery store that opened up nearby instead.

Come up with at least ten (10) different ideas for bringing business back to your store. Describe them in as much detail as you can.

Exercise 6: Snap Portraits

For each of the below, perform a short pantomime or pose yourself in a manner that clearly captures the essence of the listed personality, mood, or situation. It may help if you position yourself in front of a mirror.

Try to come up with a few different ways of demonstrating each item in the list. You can also work as a team with other people to do the exercise if you prefer.

(a) A bored commuter

(b) A prima donna

(c) The Grim Reaper

(d) Someone who is completely clueless

(e) A know-it-all

(f) Listening to an incessantly annoying sound coming from you-don't-know-where

(g) You just know trouble's brewing somewhere!

(h) Waiting for what seems like forever when you're in a hurry.

(i) An eager, unappreciated philosopher

(j) Someone who is a delight to be around

Exercise 7: Creativity in Action

Write a short commercial jingle to boost sales (which are currently in the dumps) for a horrible tasting, but miraculous and quick-acting cough syrup. Not kidding when I say that the stuff really tastes ghastly!

Exercise 8: Awareness, Sensory, and Experience

Sit for a little while among a crowd of people. Take your time and look around.

Who stands out and captures your attention the most?

Why?

Do this exercise several times at different locations.

Exercise 9: Word Play

What visuals come to mind when you hear the pseudo-phrase "totally twikitty"? Describe what you see in 50 words or more.

Exercise 10: Snap Portraits

Seek out unusual-looking buildings, displays, objects or people who are doing fascinating or thought-provoking unusual things.

Describe what you found.

If you could change it, how you would change it to make it EVEN MORE UNUSUAL?

Exercise 11: Imagination

Take your time and come up with a paragraph or two to complete each of the following phrases:

(a) Daniel always bit his tongue when …

(b) When the roof started leaking the family jumped for joy because …

(c) An incredible number of squirrels were spotted in Jack's backyard this morning ...

Exercise 12: Ideation

Elaine tripped and fell while jogging in the park on a sunny mid-summer's day and got a big gash on both her face and leg as a result, big enough that she needed lots of stitches.

Any other details about Elaine, the park, the day, and everything else are up to you to visualize.

Give yourself 20 minutes to think up at least twenty (20) possible reasons for what could have caused her to fall and hurt her face and leg.

In this exercise, the goal is to come up with as many explanations as you can AS FAST AS YOU CAN.

Exercise 13: Pictures, Patterns, and Abstractions

Draw one or more pictures or patterns (not faces or people) to visualize each of the following words or phrases:

(a) Fear

(b) Winning the lottery

(c) Boredom

(d) First day of a new job

The concept and ideas are what's most important, not the artwork.

Exercise 14: Ideation

Come up with twenty (20) "completely different from each other" uses for a ball point pen.

Exercise 15: Imagination

What is it like to be a young circus elephant?

Imagine a life for him or her.   The young elephant's circumstances, personality, and past experiences are all up to you to envision.

Exercise 16: Pictures, Patterns, and Abstractions

Draw a pattern (on paper or in your mind) that makes you think of something sad and then slowly morph it into something happy. Show the progression (all the steps) from sad to happy.

Exercise 17: Snap Solutions

You are one of two teenage best-friends in a rented boat during the off-season. The boat's oars fell into the water and sunk to the bottom (*didn't I tell ya not to monkey around with them!*). The boat is in the middle of a river 60 feet wide and is now heading towards a 10-foot waterfall. At the current rate of speed, the boat will reach the falls in about 20 minutes, but the water is becoming increasingly rough. You are both wearing life jackets. Neither of you are very experienced boaters, but your friend bragged to the boat rental person that he or she was. Your friend tends to panic easily, catastrophize, and babble incessantly in scary situations (*you love 'em anyhow*). He/she is also the only one of you that knows how to swim.

How do you and your friend get out of this situation?

How would you approach the problem? What would you be thinking about? What would you say, try (or look for) and in what order?

And assuming it's not available or feasible or your attempt fails, what would you say, try or look for next (i.e. first, I would look to see if ....).

Exercise 18: Stop and Reflect

Think of at least two or three people you know who stand out in your mind as being really creative. Why did you pick them?

Exercise 19: Pictures, Patterns, and Abstractions

For the next week, take a notepad with you wherever you go and draw a doodle at every opportunity. It doesn't have to be about anything in particular - just mindlessly doodle and let the doodle take whatever shape it wants to. When you finish each doodle, put a number next to it, giving each doodle the next highest number (1,2,3, etc.).

At the end of the week, look at your doodles. What observations can you make about them? When you look at them in order, what observations can you make? Do any patterns emerge? Did any changes take place?

Exercise 20: Thought Expression

Come up with a poem or song (at least 8 lines long) about the experience of seeing things differently.

Interpret that phrase any way you want.

Exercise 21: Word Play

All day today, in every conversation you have with anyone, somewhere in the conversation, work in the words:

"silver" and "dotted line".

Those two words have to naturally fit the flow of the conversation, not just be thrown in. Figure out how to make the conversation flow so those words make sense in it.

Exercise 22: Ideation

Come up with at least twenty (20) "completely different from each other" uses for a penny.

Exercise 23: Awareness, Sensory, and Experience

Go for a stroll outside and make note of how many different smells you come across within a 30 minute stretch of time.

For the top three (3) worst and top three (3) nicest smells, what two or three things come to mind when you smell that smell? What images does the smell evoke?

Exercise 24: Creativity in Action

From only the clothes in your wardrobe and other items you already own, put together an outfit that is the "exact opposite" of your personality and what you would normally wear (an outfit that is the least like you).

Exercise 25: Ideation

Create at least three (3) ideas/concepts for a new television series which have not been done before (to your knowledge). The concepts can be in an existing genre (i.e. comedy, reality, drama, etc.) or can be for a completely new genre that you make up.

Exercise 26: Imagination

What kinds of things do you imagine tortoises do for fun? What things would a tortoise never ever do?

Think of at least 3 or 4 things each.

Exercise 27: Awareness, Sensory, and Experience

Sit somewhere or go for a stroll and, for the people that pass by, observe where their eyes are focused.

What patterns do you notice with this?

Do this at several different locations.

Exercise 28: Snap Portraits

Seek out a portrait painting of a house or a room in a house, but not a photograph. It can be on the internet, at a museum, a store, or anywhere else. The painting must have no people in it. Also, it must not be a house you are familiar with or have even heard of.

Study it.

What vibe does the painting give off?

Based on what you see, imagine a life for the person or people who live there, and describe anything else that comes to mind when you look at it.

Exercise 29: Snap Solutions

Think up as many possible solutions as you can to the following problem:

Bayview High School has identified what they consider a growing problem.   An increasing number of students are cutting classes.

What possible things can the school do to get a better handle on the problem and/or solve it so that it is a win-win solution for all?

Exercise 30: Thought Expression

Come up with a poem or song (at least 8 lines long) about drowning.

Interpret the word any way you want.

Exercise 31: Word Play

Think of 20 words that rhyme with or are synonyms of the word "light".

Now make a sentence using at least 5 of those words.

Exercise 32: Awareness, Sensory, and Experience

Sit or walk around somewhere where there are people. Do this at different times of the day and at different locations; some locations with just a few people, some with a lot of people.

What do you notice about the moods of the different people you encounter? Similar? Lots of variations?

How would you describe the "vibe" of the location? Why?

Do you see any patterns emerging?

Did the location or the other people's moods have any effect on your own mood, energy level, or creative juices?

Exercise 33: Creativity in Action

Make up a new children's outdoor game.

Describe its rules and what ages the game would be for.

Exercise 34: Imagination

What do you envision the typical household kitchen will look like 30 years from now? How about 100 years from now?

Describe what it would have and the everyday interactions people would have with their kitchens.

Describe what's good and bad about it.

Exercise 35: Ideation

Come up with at least twenty (20) "completely different from each other" uses for a piece of string.

Exercise 36: Imagination

10-year-old Susie was in the middle of sliding down a rainbow when it suddenly parted and she slipped through it into another world.

Describe the world she sees, who if anyone is in it, and whether or how she can get back home. Or, maybe she'll decide to stay?

Exercise 37: Creativity in Action

Select a random TV show or movie (but one that you've never seen before) and watch it with the sound on mute.

For at least 10 minutes, come up with your own dialogue for what the characters are saying to each other.

Do this for a few different TV shows.

Exercise 38: Awareness, Sensory, and Experience

Listen closely to a type of music that you totally hate for a minimum of 5 minutes. Find 2 or 3 things about it or within it that are positive or that you can see would be a reason why others would like it.

Exercise 39: Ideation

A happy and very eager bride was an hour late for her own wedding.

Come up with ten (10) serious and believable reasons and ten (10) hysterically funny reasons for why she was late.

Exercise 40: Pictures, Patterns, and Abstractions

Draw a pattern or picture, using only circles of the same or varying sizes, that conveys the feeling of someone who has had one too many cups of strong coffee.

Exercise 41: Snap Portraits

Come up at least a few different explanations for each of the following:

(a) Why Allie has a phobia of coffee mugs, but strangely, not of coffee cups.

(b) Why Dino will absolutely not cut the growing mass of ivy hanging down from the lower roof, which is now obstructing the entryway to his home.

(c) Why Martha will only wear orange shoes.

(d) Why Jack, a grocery store cashier, always chuckles whenever he sees someone purchasing licorice.

(e) Why Jeffrey, who is not the least bit superstitious, will never step on cracks or seams in the sidewalk.

(f) Why the painter always leaves a small area near the center of the canvas empty.

(g) Why Becca always walks her dog precisely at midnight without fail.

(h) Why Chase always digs a small hole in his backyard each weekend.

Exercise 42: Snap Solutions

Two countries have been waging an ideological war with each other for generations and both have expressed no desire to ever be on friendly terms with each other. No one has ever been killed as a result of this war and no one has ever been physically or economically harmed. But, the tensions from it are weighing heavily on all.

Come up with as many "completely different from each other" approaches as you can for improving their situation.

Exercise 43: Creativity in Action

Come up with a short dance routine to the tune of the "Happy Birthday" song. The routine can't involve moving your legs! Your legs must remain in the same position (your choice) from the start to the end of the dance. Also, you cannot use your voice to sing, speak any "words", or hum anything.

The dance can't be comprised of just random or rhythmic movements. The dance must clearly convey a sense of your well wishes.

Exercise 44: Imagination

Take your time and come up with a paragraph or two to complete each of the following phrases:

(a) The neglected violin …

(b) I wonder whatever became of Alice because the last time I saw her …

(c) Just a few more pieces and then ...

(d) As the train left the station, Lily became alarmed ...

Exercise 45: Stop and Reflect

Reflect back on different times in your life when you applied your creativity (ingenuity, inventiveness, imagination, originality, resourcefulness, or whatever you want to call it).

Which times(s) stand out in your mind the most? Why?

Exercise 46: Creativity in Action

Make up a new word that can be used as both a noun and a verb. It should be related to something in your everyday life.

Create one or more definitions for your new word and for each definition, construct an illustrative sentence.

Now use the word all day tomorrow and explain what it means to anyone who asks. Did anyone ask? Reflect on why or why not. Try the exercise again with a new word.

Exercise 47: Thought Expression

Come up with a poem or song (at least 8 lines long) that has the words – water, deep, routine, and parlor – in it.

Exercise 48: Awareness, Sensory, and Experience

For the next week, take a completely different route to school or work or the store or wherever you usually go. No, not slightly different – completely different!

Make note of five (5) or more types of things you saw that you don't usually see on your normal route.

Exercise 49: Ideation

Your neighbor's 6-year old daughter recently lost her favorite unique-looking stuffed giraffe and she is very upset about it.

Come up with at least twenty (20) "completely different from each other" things to say or do to make her feel better.

Exercise 50: Creativity in Action

Cook something different. It should not be from an existing recipe. Challenge yourself and invent a brand new recipe. Your own creation! The only caveats are that it must have at least 10 ingredients and it can't resemble any recipe you've heard of, seen, or eaten before.

Exercise 51: Imagination

You recently discovered that your pepper shaker is upset (*yes, they do actually have feelings!*) because you pay much more attention to the salt shaker than you do to it and because you treat them both like they were just inanimate objects. The pepper shaker has a reputation in the spice community for not being very easy to convince about anything, stubborn when it comes to changing its ways, and for being somewhat revengeful at times.

Come up with a plan to make it calm down and feel better.

But beware; the pepper shaker is also very smart and intuitive.

Exercise 52: Pictures, Patterns, and Abstractions

Draw a picture of something that exists in the real world (not abstract) utilizing each of the number shapes from 0 to 9 and only those shapes. You can use any of the numbers more than once. The number shapes can be solid, dotted, curvy, block, or any other way of drawing the numbers, but it still has to be clear what number it is.

Exercise 53: Snap Solutions

You are one of 5 twenty-something-year-olds trapped in a hole in the woods that is round, 15 feet in diameter and 30 feet deep. NO ONE HAS ANY RECOLLECTION HOW THEY GOT THERE. The earth walls of the hole are wet and perfectly smooth. One person of the group reported seeing an ominous looking older man quickly stare down into the hole and then disappear. Everyone is physically uninjured. No one has a lot of muscular strength. Any electronics they had are missing. The only personal belongings they still have are their shoes and clothes, with the pockets now empty. There is one unfamiliar knapsack with a half-gallon bottle of water, a hunting knife, a couple of paperback books, one book of matches, five apples, a pen, and a pair of sunglasses. Around them are puddles of water on the very muddy ground; wet, dead leaves; a metal bucket with two small rust holes near the bottom; and a few strong tree branches. From what they can tell it looks like its mid-morning and the sun is shining.

How would you proceed to assess the situation further to find a way for everyone to escape from the hole with as little harm as possible? What would you look for? What would you do or try first, second, third, etc?

Exercise 54: Word Play

Write one or two sentences about taking a trip to the store. Each word should start with one of the last four letters of the previous word. The sentences don't have to be grammatically correct, but they do need to make sense.

Exercise 55: Awareness, Sensory, and Experience

Close your eyes and closely listen to / scan your surroundings for at least 5 minutes. What do you hear? What are the faintest sounds you hear? What are the loudest sounds you hear? What's the most unusual sound you hear?

Try this several times at different locations, some with people and some without.

Exercise 56: Creativity in Action

You've been put in charge of planning a birthday party for a man who is turning 30 years old in August. He is married with two children, ages five and eight. They live in a small mansion situated on a large estate. In addition to the spacious grounds, the property has an Olympic size swimming pool. Money is no object and the guests will be a mix of about 200 relatives, friends, and business associates. There will be an even mix of ages attending the party and the ages of the guests will range from 5 to 85. The party needs to be memorable; one which will make the partygoers remark that they've never heard of or seen anything like it before; one the guests will remember for years to come and where all will be able to participate in the festivities and have a good time and not feel left out. There is more than enough time to plan and prepare, so no rushing to get things done would be necessary.

Come up with at least three (3) different parties (they can't resemble each other). For each, describe your plan for the party from beginning to end.

Exercise 57: Ideation

Come up with at least three (3) different ways to fully cook pasta (that don't involve boiling it in a pot of water).

Hint: the ways don't have to be practical. They just need to get the job done.

Exercise 58: Imagination

For as long as anyone can remember, planet Xeon has been cold all the time, very windy and dusty, and the light from its sun low. There is very little that is green in the landscape, but there is much vegetation. There is an abundance of small creatures and microscopic life which live in harmony with the people.

Describe what the people look like. Describe a typical day in the life of a citizen of planet Xeon, including what their homes and home life are like.

Exercise 59: Pictures, Patterns, and Abstractions

Create one or more patterns or pictures to visualize each of the following words:

(a) Chaos

(b) Bliss

(c) Loyalty

(d) Hunger

(e) Patience

The concept and ideas are what's most important, not the artwork.

Exercise 60: Creativity in Action

For the next week or so, challenge yourself to style your hair in five (5) or more "completely different" styles from the typical style(s) you usually arrange your hair in. And don't forget to take a photo!

Printed in Great
Britain
by Amazon